T0103935

STOP
Chronic Back Pain in as Little as 3 Weeks

My secret, life-transforming method, to feel free from buttock, leg, and spine pain, caused by back problems.

Thomas De Tremblay

This book is part of a "Self Help" series.

Look forward to, new, up coming writings; poems; Christian Revelations; Eternal Boundless Love vs. The So Called Nothing of Science; Philosophy of Man; Theological Lacking in the Church and Fleeting Affections.

For more information go to mindrattler.com

WESTBOW®
PRESS
A DIVISION OF THOMAS NELSON
& ZONDERVAN

WestBow Press books may be ordered through
booksellers or by contacting:

WestBow Press
A Division of Thomas Nelson & Zondervan
1663 Liberty Drive
Bloomington, IN 47403
www.westbowpress.com
1-(866) 928-1240

ISBN: 978-1-4908-0170-4 (sc)
ISBN: 978-1-4908-0171-1 (e)

Library of Congress Control Number: 2013912621

Printed in the United States of America.

WestBow Press rev. date: 3/21/2014

Dedication

This book is dedicated to my wife and all those who will be blessed and helped by it.

From the many ways one may help

I chose this one

It may seem humble

Its impact, I am sure

Is a blessing to those who read this book

And I hope they take to heart,

The proven method set forth in it

God bless all of you

Thomas De Tremblay

The Book That Had To Be Written

I wrote the book
I did not want it to be a vain pursuit
I found what I knew as fact
I sent it out
I made it my small mission
If it could help in any way,
I surely would find the motivation.
I do not crave fortune
I just want to please Him in all I do
I remember the goal set before me
It was not an easy task
The reward is worth it
A simple thing
A blessing for some
Hopefully for the many.

Thomas De Tremblay

A few steps to take and you will feel better.

For those of us,
all through out the
world, who have
shared the same
pain that only we
can understand.

Perhaps, we can
help each other.

About The Author

The author lives in Canada with his lovely wife of 35 years. He has a son in the Canadian Air Force. He is a business entrepreneur, a home builder, a writer and a musician. He has a self help series that reaches out to educate people who are willing to hear and practice what he lives by and he dedicated his life and is motivated by his need to help others.

I had a procedure done on my spine, in the hospital, in my early 20's, at which time I had to lay down for approximately one month to recover. I had to live with a 20 lb. limit on my back for almost 40 years, and for the last 15 of those years, I discovered a complete method of well being to relieve and live without back pain. Because of this experience, I humbly feel qualified to pass on this valuable information to help others.

Thomas De Tremblay

Table of Contents

Introduction

I have kept this book length to a minimum, to simplify it, as not to bore the reader. I have condensed the valuable information, always keeping in mind, to never miss the point, but to make the contents easier to read and I also made sure to have it in large print for those of us who always wished that everything was written larger.

I kept in mind the reasons why someone would pick up a book of this kind. As far as I am concerned, I have always felt it is a duty to pass on anything that I, over the years, came to master. This book is no different, and I might add, this is very important to me, the sharing of this knowledge, that I have practiced over the years. The goal in it self, is worth it indeed.

For years I was living with a chronic back condition. It can be a struggle for those of us who have to live with this condition. At the onset of a flare up, the pain is a constant reminder of the days and weeks to come. You will be conscious of a discomfort in the neck, or the back, or your behind, down the legs and sometimes down to your knees and feet.

CHAPTER 1

The Importance of Your Back

Joe

Joe was a dry wall installer and taper and he worked for himself. In order to produce more, and get ahead, he was twisting his body incorrectly, while lifting. Time was money. Later on in life he paid for it. He had to live with a constant pain in his lower back. He was happy to find out that he could get operated on and if it was successful, the pain would be gone, but he was also told of the dangers in such an operation. He had the procedure and it was successful. Now he works, but he has not given up the bad habits, so he will certainly be back on the operating table again, which will make it impossible for him to do any hard physical work again. Please read on.

How can I stress the importance of you being good to your back? By now you know and probably think it is too late to undo the damage, but you will have to make a conscious choice, if you want to resume your life as it was at one time and it is also important for you to realize that you will never be the same even if you come to a point at which time the pain is gone. You will feel safe and might think that you are out of the woods. Many like us have felt secure at one time, but we had to find out that the reality is, that once you had an episode, you will always have a weakness in your back. It is better to accept the facts as they are, then you can proceed to live in accordance with it, but there is hope that you will feel better if you take charge of your circumstance. As apposed to before, or after an episode, when you felt helpless, you will feel hopeful. Do not waste your precious time feeling sorry for yourself and know that there is always some hope and this gives you the motivation to make things better. I myself remember so many people with the glare in their eyes when they talked about their back pain and you can see how miserable they feel, when they think that it hasn't been life as usual for them, since this awful pain became part of their daily life. It crept in and robbed them of much of their happiness. That is why I wrote this book, in hope that they try and implement some of the things I have written about, but as it was for me, we want a pill or a quick fix. It is hard to accept that science has not come up with a simple solution but it is our lack of understanding that is partly the problem. So we do not have to linger in pain if we take charge and make it our business to help ourselves because in the long run, it is your own pain. No one else feels it and very few can understand what it is like to live with back problems. Many times people think that a back problem is a muscle problem and unless they have it themselves they can never understand what it is all about. For young and old, the story is the same.

This method which I have developed works, but it is not a guarantee for everyone.

CHAPTER 2

When Did It Happen?

Julie

Julie loved snow boarding on high ski hills, but one day while going down hill she hit a patch of ice and went flying and landed on her back. From that time on, she lived with a constant pain in her lower back. It took years for the pain to go away, through physiotherapy and she had to give up snow boarding, which she enjoyed so much, just because of a fall. Now she is careful in everything she does because she knows, one slip, and the pain will be back. Please read on.

It all started with me, when one winter I slid on the ice at the young age of 19 years old. Not long after that I felt a long persisting pain in the left part of my behind. It was deep inside the buttock. At that time in my life I was not accustomed to any lingering pain, especially when I didn't know the cause, or the remedy. So to erase this uncomfortable feeling, when I was sitting down for a long time, my way to deal with this pain was to stand up and even when I was standing, I still could feel it deep inside, but it gave me a little relief at the time. I thought, and guessed, that the problem was in the bone because it was deep inside the buttock. Some months later, little did I know, I found out and was told by specialists, that what I had done, was injured a disc, or to be more precise, had crushed a spacer between the discs. So you could say that the nerve was inflamed and touching the spacer causing the different pains.

CHAPTER 3

That Pain!

John

John was a strong man and took pride in lifting heavy loads. He was the lumber jack, the tough guy, but one day while moving a log out of the way, without adjusting his body position, he yelled out in pain, in a second, his life changed for the worse. He had to be rushed to the hospital and not long after had to be operated on his back. He still brags about his strength but when it comes to his back, it's another story. He knows now that it's too late for him and strength itself is there but if you misuse it you can lose the ability to use it again. Please read on.

There it was the year had come and gone, the pain was constant, drove me mad and there was no way to relieve it. I was sent to a back specialist. He manipulated my spine and found out where the problem was with his finger. He said that I needed some work done on my back. A month later, I was in the hospital on a special table and I was on the way to get a very painful intervention. I was to suffer a long and thick needle entering my spine or to be more precise, between the vertebrae and to what felt like a penetration in a thick nerve; at least it felt like that. It was a painful experience that I would not wish on anyone else. It took me one month to recover from it, in bed. Unknown to me, I was not to stand up or I would get sick to my stomach in a burst impossible to stop and the pressure in my head was unbearable. The cause of this condition was a fluid that was injected in my spine and I had felt it going all the way up, inside to the back of my head.

This was the cause or the reason why I could not get up or stay up very long, before it hit me real hard and I would get sick to my stomach.

CHAPTER 4

Hope In The End

Charlotte

Charlotte had an office job. It was pleasant, air conditioned in the summer, comfortable in the winter months and she loved her job. Her boss was a pleasant man and her co-workers were all friends, but one thing everyone did complain about, was the sitting all day. It was uncomfortable, so they asked their boss if he could possibly change the chairs and purchase chairs with more back support. By that time, Charlotte, had been having back pain for the past couple of years. It was becoming a burden to bear, but soon as the new chairs came in, to everyone's surprise, after a few weeks, they all noticed that their pain had vanished. Please read on.

A month later and this time, I was able to stand up and to stay up for good and the symptoms were gone, thank God for that. It was only the beginning; I understood by then, that I was never going to be the same again. I was told I could not lift more than 20lbs ever. I had to make a living in my field, so I lifted very heavy loads in order to advance financially in life to my detriment. Even though I was careful, to bend my knees, a little slip, and there it was back in full force.

CHAPTER 5

Don't Lift Heavy Loads or Over Reach

Bill

Bill had always worked hard, so this was just another day, so he thought. He went to work on his job sight and a fellow worker asked Bill for his help to move a heavy machine about a foot from where it stood. Always happy to help, Bill rushed and lifted his end of the machine. At that moment he felt a strange sensation but kept on lifting. When they put the machine down, Bill felt a pain in his back, he dismissed it and carried on as usual, but when he drove home, he felt another pain in his bottom which he had to live with from then on, but there is still hope for him. Please read on.

From then on, if I turned the wrong way or reached too high, or lifted anything heavy, I would pay for it and I always did. So now I had to worry about the pain coming back at any time, if I made one mistake. As I said before I had to provide for myself and at the time I was not insured by the government and I could not get insured because of my back. I had to learn to be doubly cautious just about everything I did. Every time I lifted a heavy load without bended knees, I paid for it. The other thing that will get you in trouble is lifting and twisting at the same time. You must turn your body around, don't twist. You could say that I am a lucky man or that I beat the odds. Many times, I came close to never recovering.

CHAPTER 6

Who Will Listen?

Richard

Richard was working at a summer job as a landscaper but the job required one to lift rolls of sod and rock and a lot of shoveling was involved. He needed the money, so he took the job. It was a tough job, either in the sun or the rain. They had hired him right on the spot and he was told to just follow the other guys and pitch in. There was no training at all, as to how to lift properly without injuring yourself. The constant, improper, lifting caught up to him. He finished his day, but when he came home, he fell asleep on his couch and when he woke up, he was in pain and his back was hurting him. He could hardly walk, so that was the end of that job for him, but he stills pays the price of discomfort until this day. Please read on.

The story takes a different twist, as the years went by, I have to say, as for most of us and I am talking here about the various people I talk to, it's the same problem for everyone and we are mostly ignorant as to how to relieve that pain and if we go to a doctor, they usually are helpless as to what they can do for you, except operate on you, at the cost of your flexibility. They will suggest, sometimes, to wear a support belt around your lower back, but the one thing that we often ignore is the literature they give us that clearly tells us how to sleep, how to sit and how to lift objects, but somehow we just don't believe that it can change the situation, because unknown to us, we don't understand the thinking behind the literature.

CHAPTER 7

The Problem

Fred

Fred had been active all of his life. There was nothing he could not do. He enjoyed all sports, from boxing to water skiing and everything in between. One day, while jogging on a paved road, Fred tripped and fell. As a result, he hurt his back. He went to a chiropractor, but he could not lose the pain. Out of desperation, he had an operation. He felt better, but he lost flexibility and shrunk a little. He will never be the same, and he does not accept that yet. He has not changed his bad habits in his everyday life, in spite of him having a weakness in his back now. Please read on.

Up until now, I have talked about the problem and have not explained the way to lose that pain or that if you do lose the pain for a while, what I have discovered, over many years, it will come back but you too can free yourself of the lingering pain and protect yourself so that you will not cause anymore damage and have to live a crippled life when you're old. For those of us, who have experienced the pain, we seek never to have it again, but it comes and goes and there is something we can do about it.

CHAPTER 8

It Is Partly Your Own Doing

Paul

Paul had been out of work for years, due to his back condition. He learned how to live with it, but over the years, got addicted to pain killers. He felt he needed them to numb the pain and it did, but as time went on, he needed them, not only for the pain, but also for his dependency. No one had shown him how he could ease the pain and no one took the time to help him understand his back condition and how to live in accordance to it. He did the best he could to go on, but now he is addicted, still has the pain, and to make things worse, his wife left him because of his addiction. It is a sad story, indeed. Please read on.

What does it all mean? It is clear to me that most of us are responsible for our further pain and discomfort. I will try to explain in more depth, what could possibly do further damage to our back. Let us discuss clothing for a moment. I am always surprised to see people with back problems, wearing tight close around the waist, especially with a belt that crushes the lower back. It is important to get an understanding of the spine, if we are going to get better. The spine has to be in a natural position and it is very obvious that when you look at cowboy cut jeans, for example, and belt and buckle, it crams the behind and lower spine. It should not be worn at all. A looser fitting is called for if you want to have an intelligent strategy, so loose the belt. You will thank me later. I wear pants with an elastic waist.

CHAPTER 9

Take Note

Anthony

Anthony was a chef in a busy kitchen. He was always working on a hard concrete floor, so over the years he developed pain in his legs and heels and back. It became so severe that he had to contemplate a different career, but someone suggested that he should work in a different restaurant that had a wood floor with some flex to it. So he transferred to a different work place and now worked on a soft, wood floor and now he feels much better. Then he realized that if he had proper shoes for working, it would make things even better. He purchased shoes which were designed for his type of job, from a health store. So for Anthony, once he got the proper shoes and the proper working environment, after taking control of his situation, even if he still has problems, he made his life better and he did not have to abandon the career he loves. Please read on.

Therefore, you must look at every activity that you choose to do on a daily basis. This might sound like a chore, but in the end, you again will thank me, if you can give it a little bit of your attention. Try to identify things that you can do and some that you should never do. For example, we should never go jogging, especially on a hard surface because even if you do not feel it now, you are actually doing further damage and you will feel it when you are old, if not before. I will say that you should loose the hard running all together, period. Your best option is to walk and walk properly. There are books to explain how to walk in a safe manner. Your shoes should be comfortable, not too cushiony, or not too hard. The rule for me is this; running shoes are out. They do not fit the foot properly. It is natural for the foot to be fitted, with let's say, a comfortable real European shoe of yester year, with a small heel and a firm sole, and I always wear leather shoes because they do breath, but this part is mostly for comfort. If you wear running shoes, you should where the more natural type, but this is up to you. I have come up with a complete system for my self that works and suggest you do the same. It does work for me and I have no choice, but to abide by my understanding of the problem and the solution.

We have always been told that if you have strong stomach muscles, that it will relieve some stress on the spine, which is true, but this book is not about losing weight to feel better, but about feeling better in your own situation, regardless of your weight. Naturally, if you get into better, physical, condition, this will further benefit you.

CHAPTER 10

Do Not Run To a Chiropractor Every Time You Think It Will Help You

Rick

Rick was a chiropractor and had worked on people's back for years and even though he shared in their suffering, from their back pain, he himself did not fully comprehend what they were going through, until it happened to him. One afternoon, out of the blue, when he was lifting something in the yard, he felt a weird pain in his lower back and the pain persisted. He tried to relieve the pain, but he was told by a specialist that what he needed was an operation. He did not accept the diagnostic, so he tried anyway to fix the pain through his knowledge in his practice, but to no avail. Eventually he had to have the operation on his back and now if someone comes to him, he really knows the feeling and he wishes everyone could be free from the pain as he is. Now, if he thinks you need an operation on your back, he will tell you. Please read on.

Chiropractic won't always help and if it does and when it does, you're chancing pinching the nerve further as I heard from people that had to suffer after and as I was told by a chiropractor, some people do need an operation. I myself have used them before and I will explain what happened to me and why you should be cautious. Here's why; once I got up with a burning sensation down the leg. I went to a chiropractor, he worked on my back and the burning went away. I was very happy. He told me to come back the week after, so I did. He worked on my back again and the burning came back, worse. A week later, I went back again and he cracked my back again, the pain left and this time I never went back; a lesson well taken. I could have done the same by doing what I have learned myself, with my method. After years of ignorance as to what is happening when you pinch the nerve, you have to see it this way. It is inflamed, it touches the disk or the spacing between the disk, so if you leave it and do not stress it further and most importantly, do not compound the injury and if you know how to relieve and rest the spine, that's when you find out that nature itself, remedies, with time. I am not speaking here of a devastating blow to the spine or a crushed vertebrae, but for 90% of us, we can eliminate the pain by eliminating the cause in the first place.

CHAPTER 11

A Bad Memory

Shane

Shane was a contractor and use to working physically. He never had problems when he worked as an interior contractor but it took on a turn for the worse because he went into the siding business. There was a lot of reaching, lifting in awkward positions, and going up ladders with weight on your shoulders. He pinched a nerve in his back. He was one of the lucky ones; he got better after some time of being more careful of his movements and resting more and some luck, but he will never forget that awful feeling of pain in his spine which he lived with for months. Shamus did not relieve his pain because he understood how to relieve it, but because he happened to mirror what I am teaching you and of what I am writing about in this book. Please read on.

I clearly recall, years ago when I lifted a canoe and I flipped it over. At once I felt a sharp and weird sensation in my back and I heard like a detaching of my back muscles and I was sure at that moment, so I thought, this one is the big one because I was told years ago that I would probably need a further operation due to the weakness in my spine, sort of speak. After that episode, I had to try this time to find by any means possible, a way to relieve this new awful pain. I never depended on medication before because I was told by doctors that it would only mask the pain and never would go to the root of the problem and that I could get addicted as many are to pain killers. Never the less, for some people it is necessary. I had to try to lie on my back with my knees up but you can only do that for so long, so I set out to sleep on my side like a fetus and turn on each side when I got restless. I did that for three weeks. Mysteriously the pain left when I got up one morning. It was gone as quickly as it came. It was not easy to sleep on your side, when you are accustomed to sleep on your back or on your belly and I was conscious of the uncomfortable sideway position for many nights when I tried to sleep, and it felt for me like I would never enjoy the new sleeping position. I persisted and this is the secret. You eventually sleep and you turn back and forth all night and eventually it will become your, new, natural way of sleeping. After a few years, I realized that I get a better rest if I hug a pillow between my arms, which rests my arm and my shoulder. Now when you have an episode of back problem due to something you did wrong in the day, it is better not to sleep with your legs extended, for a while as to help the spine to relax. I think the idea of all of this is to always relax the spine to give it a rest in the fetus position or at least on the side slightly crunched. If you want to and can bear a pillow between your legs, it's also fine, but I find it was more of a bother and for me it did not make a difference, not to say it doesn't help. It is something I can't get use to but if someone is patient, it would definitely bring relief more quickly. I suggest that if you experience some pain, because you sat incorrectly, or over reached, or lifted incorrectly, to use the method at all times in your life.

CHAPTER 12

Sitting In a Vehicle

Marion

Marion had the dream job of delivering mail by car to rural areas, but as the years went by she always had to modify her movements because of the reaching out and constant repetitious work. So it was not unusual for her to go home in pain. Eventually the struggle to work became unbearable due to her back pain. After months of therapy and no hope in sight, she went on disability and that is after months of fighting with the government and insurance companies. Now she stays home and wishes she could resume her work or do something else, but about 90% of jobs involve sitting or standing for long periods of time, which she can no longer do because of her back problem. Ultimately she wishes to lose the pain. Please read on.

Now when you sit in a vehicle, there is added stress to your spine from the bouncing when driving on rough roads. The best thing I ever did, which I was never told by a doctor or a chiropractor, was to purchase a good back support. The back support which can be purchased at most drugstores, placed behind your back gives your back firm support in a vehicle where it is needed the most, no matter how short of time you are in it. It takes no time at all, to stress your spine in a vehicle. The nerve in your spine needs some relief and if you use this method and make this your new way of life, you will never look back and wonder why you never used one before. You will feel the difference very quickly. I am always telling people with back problems, to invest in a good quality back support, designed for that very purpose.

CHAPTER 13

How To Sleep and Sit Properly

Edward

Edward was a heavy set man and he always slept on his back or his belly. As he grew old, he put even more weight on and gradually it became uncomfortable to sleep on his belly, so most of the time he slept on his back. He had the same mattress and bed for years and he sunk into his mattress in the waist area. Over time, he developed a sore back, until he realized that maybe it was time for a new mattress. As he shopped around, Edward was told that his problem was caused by his bed, because the springs were sagging, so he either had to get a box spring and a mattress or put plywood underneath his new mattress and that, he was told, would definitely help and it did. Please read on.

How do you sleep? Many of us do not understand that the spine needs to rest, just like your mind and the rest of your body. It is common sense but it's easy to forget. So you need to rest your spine, whenever you have an opportunity to do so. Whether you sit, or lie down, or go to sleep, you should do it all, according to my method. I will explain what I mean by all of this. Do not sit on a couch or a chair with a soft cushion; it's the worse thing you can do. It only takes minutes and you undo hours of spine rest. You should use a back support when sitting in your home for better support. I have one that stays in the car and one inside when I sit. My wife also has one in the car. You must sit upright in a straight position, with your back straight. Always remember when you're sitting, to make a conscious decision to sit straight and I mean on a solid chair. With a back support you can relax your back without having to worry if you are sitting properly. Just make sure to adjust the back support to your back until it feels comfortable. You should always have a firm cushion. You should never sink into a chair or a couch. The seat has to be supporting your spine all the way down to your bottom. For prolonged amounts of time when watching TV, you must and you should, always lie down sideways and change the position from one end of the couch to the other, when you get restless. Support your head, so your head will be comfortable and your neck is aligned with your spine. Do not have your head too high. If at all possible, never, lie on your back or your belly. It has the opposite effect of what you think it is doing for you. It is the hardest thing for people to accept but it is a fact, that lying on your back or belly, will never solve the problem as I explained earlier in the book.

CHAPTER 14

I Feel Good

Fernando

Fernando was a truck driver. It was a way of life for him. It wasn't strenuous but there were hours and hours of sitting in a truck. Even though the seats had shock absorbers, the fact that he was sitting for hours, eventually weakened his back. After years of touring and millions of miles, he was told he could no longer do his job; you guessed it; unless he gets an operation. Obviously, this was difficult for Fernando because he had to provide for his family. You have now seen a pattern in all these stories. I stress the fact and keep reminding you, there are not many choices out there, to stop your back pain. These are the facts. The stories are all different, but the results remain the same. We want to eliminate the factors that are causing the problem in the first place. This book is about hope once you have, unfortunately, become one of the statistics. My wish is that this book will help the many people like Fernando and the others. Please read on

You can feel better after doing these things, you can finally be happy in your life and you're not always going to feel this constant pain in your body, you will be like everybody else and you can enjoy your life. I hope you try and give it at least 3 weeks to find out that one day you get up and you don't feel the pain. You will learn quickly after this, when you make a mistake, but at least you can feel better, that as soon as you feel the pain again, you apply the method and get relief again. You should always check with your doctor to make sure you haven't crushed the vertebrae, but you should always have hope along with your physician, that it is not going to be a prolonged situation, because either way, you will always live with the method. I found that for me, if I live this way and I apply this, the pain eventually goes.

CHAPTER 15

Be Happy and Rest

What are we to get out of all of this? I could say that persistence in doing the right things allows a pay off and patience is a must if you want to be relieved from the pain and as the saying always says, "Rest is always the answer when it comes to health".

I hope for you that this will bless you and believe, it has done this for me. I lived with this for 40 years. This book does not replace a doctor, but as a man who cares and lived with this problem, I am certainly qualified to add to the council of a practitioner.

Testimony

My wife was complaining for a couple months that she had a pain in her back. She use to say it was probably cancer because of stories she heard before at her work place but for some reason I never had a clue that perhaps my wife would have the same problem as I had so by putting my hand and fingers on her spine, I felt a vertebrae with a slight protrusion. I massaged the area carefully and she said it felt better, so I knew then, as many times before, when I asked my wife to do the same to me, that it took the pain away for a brief moment. So firstly I told her that she should sleep sideways when she laid and watched TV, I had to constantly remind her to move back and forth. We bought a back support for her and in her case it only took two weeks for the pain to go away. She could not believe that my method could actually work for her, but now she is a believer. So by giving it a chance, the pain vanished, just as it came. Now she will not be in the car without a back support. Thank God that you can buy something so well engineered, as a back support and yet it is such a simple concept and it does more than anyone can ever hope, for your back. So for those people that drive a vehicle without it, and they wonder why they have back problems, I say, "Do not drive without a back Support". People are not made for sitting for prolonged periods of time. As our society has come to take us off of our natural settings, it's no wonder why we have created so many problems and we fail to recognize how to fix it, because we are not used to question our own situations any longer and we fail to realize the difference in the way we live our daily lives as apposed to years gone by. This is a fact of our life now and not too many recognize the unnatural way we live and how it affects us all. So now we can do something about this, at least, if we take one thing at a time and find the cause and the solution. I hope it will do for you, what it has done for us.

Closing Thoughts

How many times have I hoped,

answers from doctors, but to no avail

The response is always the same

Medicate, don't lift, or get an operation

But for us, it is not the answer we seek

We want a clear and quick fix

Unfortunately, there is none

But hope is the best medicine.

With the help of God, reason and science,

we can find peace and comfort.

Amen

Thomas De Tremblay

The Gift

What a blessing, the many days we enjoy

So much love, yet never enough time

When we take hold of life

The beauty and serenity of it all

In adversity, even then we see

The sun shines upon all

Our friends go about their business

While we ourselves wait patiently

There is another world in hiding

One day it will burst forth and overtake this one

The longing of our souls finally comes

What was once just a dream has become

When the time arrives our peace will prevail

We live in hope with a light in our heart

There is a gathering to come

The freedom we seek was never of this world

Even so, we always taste of it's goodness

Among the many gifts, one shines

We partake of abundant life

The gift we take with us into eternity

It was bought at a heavy price

All we did, is accept it and take it

Our brothers and sisters gather for the love feast

They answered the call and came by the millions

They brought with them, their own gifts

A new song was heard in the distance

Their voice as beautiful as the Holy One

The melody was written long ago

The chosen were all asleep

While God was long suffering in Jesus

As he pays the price

Thomas De Tremblay

mindrattler.com

Find more poems and writings and upcoming Self Help series.

For all the good willed people of the world, that we may become one with Him.

Please read on.

The SON

The Cathedral of our mind

Its steeple in the clouds

The beauty of the Word

So much to share

Eternal Love

The destiny of it all

Thomas De Tremblay

Finally, The Answers To The Big God Questions!

All This Time, You Thought There Were No Answers

Over fifty years of mind crunching, ready to be passed on and you will never think the same after this. After you have tapped into the mind of the **MindRattler**, you will know for sure, thru reasonable truth, that the Eternal God exists and created all things. The world denies and covers the truth. It filters all new discoveries and hides in a denial of a fundamental fact, that Jesus Christ, is the Eternal God and I have taken on the task to prove it and I will back up my claim.

About Me

It all started at the young age of 8 years old, with a question that came to my mind, why am I me and not someone else. I felt separated from a whole. I have been haunted by the whys and why nots, using "the creative process" of the mind and by the help of the Holy Spirit in its various gifts given, the **mindrattler.com** came about. A writer; rock/blues musician; song writer, life long entrepreneur, inventor, deep thinker and debater of truth.

Inquire about the series of Self Help Books

The man behind the **mindrattler.com** challenges us on all fronts. Find answers to your questions about; The, So Called, Nothing of Science, The Illusiveness of Time and It's Implication in The Big Picture, Insight Into The Expanse of Matter, What's All The Fuss About Dimensional Realities?, Conflicting Religions and Their False Dogmas, and A Simplified Philosophy for Laymen.

Put The Mindrattler to the test. Find out for yourself; have any questions go to **mindrattler. com** or email me at Thomasdetremblay@gmail. com

The Storm Before The Calm

Prepare to be shaken to your beliefs, but all to a positive end. I hope it will only reinforce what you already know in your core and your reasoning and at the same time evaporate the walls that we all build around ourselves. We blind ourselves to our own true selves, to our detriment. Whether you are an atheist, a scientist, or a religious adherent, you should know that we all fall prey to the so called teachers and their repetition and duplicity of their understanding of works of all sorts that went before. The outcome of the sharing of this work is not to teach how to think but to ponder with our mind, not out of constraint by our culture, our upbringing and the thinking past on by the so called elitist mind set.

The fear is the same. We feel powerless at any new and perhaps different conclusion as to what might be true and what most of the time is false, but rest assured that if that you do know the truth, you will certainly not shrivel because as you know the truth has made you free.

What The World Failed To Give

A pursue that fails to give it a meaning

A spider of dead end roads

A climb and a slide to no where

The veil and the beauty it hides

Many miles and yet no end in sight

The cross road and the choices we made

There is a time to reflect and it could be painful

We find ourselves waiting and wanting

We try the same, over and over, but to no avail

The projects and plans we made

And so few we have accomplished

The simple things are still for free

But we paid a heavy price

All the years of our lonely life are filled with struggles

So we eat and drink, and pursue love

Little do we know there is a harbor

The wave can only carry us so far

We are solidly attached to our anchor

And it is pegged in

Never the less, it is never a walk in the park

And in the end, we are back where we began

At once we feel at peace and yet the world is
    still at war.

Thomas De Tremblay

We Meet and Come Together
The Words Become A
Chain That Binds

A curious and inquiring mind is the tool
afforded to anyone but because it is free, it
is seldom expanded on and many times it is
discouraged by ones entourage. So for someone
to expand their understanding of the various
mysteries of life and of reality, one must break
thru the constraints of every day life and pursue
knowledge of the right kind alone and as many
years in this pursuit as proven, it will leave the
pursuer often in his own world and most of the

time frustrated. As experience has proven, time and time again, all great inspirations and all of men's creations and discoveries were brought into the world at great cost to the creators, the thinkers, and the inventors. You could as one of many, if you look at your own life, find that anything great of any value in your existence has come only by, you being singled out as a non conforming individual. Whether emotionally or spiritually or in practical reality, this now makes up your very personality and that forms in you the image of yourself. For some of us it came at a price but in the long run we can not deviate from it. It is not a choice, but is more like a need that defines our longing and our happiness, regardless if people regard your place in society, trying as they do, to define you and not as you yourself, came to fully tap into your given ability and the various gifts within your own personality.

For me, as a seeker in my own journey, I have come to a conclusion, as to whether a man or a woman should live by theory and pass down limited understanding of all that pertains to life

I say no, I do not easily and never allow another to dictate to me in their limited capacity the right to filter all the great possibilities that lays in my own mind, after all it is not theirs, and this I fought throughout my life, I have met this kind of dismissing of my yearning as if they can bottle me up and shut me up so as not to rock their world,

That is how the Mind Rattler comes to realization and at this point, now because of my non ceasing inquiry mind, I have come with the help from the Giver to great conclusions about things that for most of us stay unanswered. After more than 52 years of realization and philosophizing, I can demonstrate in all logical reasoning truth that can only be refute by those of the same group, who all thru my life were hindering such a quest. They can be found at all levels of society and most of the time they hide in cloak of intelligence, but they deny the fundamental rule that will bring one to complete understanding and as history has shown throughout, that these truths have been denied yesterday, today and surely tomorrow but these truths now, many of them have finally, now been proven facts and not only theories.

I endeavor to share my objections and at times my adherence to what I would call infiltrations of new and old evolutionary and reaffirming truths that were always there and at times so simple and yet so complex.

I set out to pass on, as I have always done, in my own capacity, I have shared with those that were inclined to think that far, but I have to admit now, if I look back, I can see that a man can only absorb a certain amount of information, as to his desire, his will and his honesty and to his station in life as to whether he cares to know or if it would be any use to him. For some, complex thoughts are to be left for others to figure out, but I am not of those who shrink, but push forward and cannot be stopped.

To simplify as to not bore the reader, because there is a more pleasant side to me and perhaps, not to turn away those that I am trying to free, I will proceed to come back to a more specific discourse and explain what is meant by all this in a poetic form.

Whether one looks for love, as a pie in the sky

In truth it is where we find it

The rain falls and we bath in it

The ocean can not constrain it

The drops can not be counted

Many will have you believe

One day, perhaps they say we will

We partake of the eternal presence

But many deny their very existence

Knowledge can not be bought

For as far the eye can see

One may wonder

At the end of the rainbow

Wait the outcome of all things

The truth is space less

The future is an elusion

The past weighs us down

We can barely see

And it holds us back

At the end of our journey

We all know the same

In the betweens, lie our struggles

For some, to live, is to die to self

For others, to die to self, is death

Thomas De Tremblay

The Challenge, The Debate, The books to come

For more about things of great value, the destiny of all the good willed people of the world, contact the Mind Rattler at mindrattler.com or by email, Thomasdetremblay@gmail.com

Thomas De Tremblay

The Narrow Path

If I am on the road less traveled, am I alone?

If I look to the sky do I see heaven?

Many days will come and go but I will live for ever.

Some will meet me at the cross road and ask me for something to eat, I will always have plenty to share.

If their road is ascending, I will urge them to go on and finish the climb.

When darkness comes, I take my sword and I cut thru the maze and like in the days of old when I took my pledge, I rescue those in need.

In a vision I can see them clearly when they fight with there left hand. God is with me and I can see who is on his right side.

Some have written them off when they saw them peeking in but I saw them turning back at the site of horror and the stench of those on the inside, but we were the only ones who heard the voice of Jesus.

It was like thunder when he spoke; the earth shook; we pulled all those falling in and at the cross road the gate closed to never open again until judgment day.

Sadness engulfed us when we heard the gnashing of teeth behind the gate.

We were together when the trumpet sounded and we saw Him coming in the clouds of glory and we were caught up to be with Him forever.

Thomas De Tremblay

Diamonds and Pearls

We waited and it tarried
But we kept on knocking
The gate was shut tight
But there was always a glimpse
When the time came
A command was given
And the veil was removed
But ever so slightly
We were filled with praise
It was as He said
And it came to pass
Everything became new
The water once again turned into wine
And in our spirit we were elated
It finally came
Our mind was opened on high
The longing dissipated
Questions came to nothing
Answers became a treasure chest
At once we were not ourselves
But had become one with Him

Thomas De Tremblay